# Contents

# ⚽ The World Cup Final

The ball is flying through the air. The striker pulls back his foot. He's going to shoot! Defenders race towards the ball, but they're too late. The striker hits his shot and it curves towards the goal.

Paul May

# *Football*

This book belongs to

## OXFORD
### UNIVERSITY PRESS

Great Clarendon Street, Oxford OX2 6DP

Oxford University Press is a department of the University of Oxford.
It furthers the University's objective of excellence in research, scholarship,
and education by publishing worldwide in

Oxford  New York

Auckland  Bangkok  Buenos Aires  Cape Town  Chennai
Dar es Salaam  Delhi  Hong Kong  Istanbul  Karachi  Kolkata
Kuala Lumpur  Madrid  Melbourne  Mexico City  Mumbai  Nairobi
São Paulo  Shanghai  Taipei  Tokyo  Toronto

Oxford is a registered trade mark of Oxford University Press
in the UK and in certain other countries

Text copyright © Paul May 2003

The moral rights of the author and artist have been asserted

First published 2003

Paperback ISBN 0–19–910928–1

1  3  5  7  9  10  8  6  4  2

Printed in Spain

Acknowledgments
Photographs: *Photodisc* title page, title verso, 4, 20tr, 24;
*Action plus* 5, 6-7, 14-15, 20bl, 22l, 23, 25, 27, 28, 29; *EMP* 9, 12-13, 16-17, 17tr, 21, 26;
*Mikail Sipovitch* 18-19

Illustrations: *Chris Brown* 10-11

The goalkeeper leaps...
stretches out his fingers... and **SAVES!**

**The World Cup Final has begun.**

In the stadium, a hundred thousand people cheer and yell. Around the world, a thousand million people cheer and yell.

All over the world, people are watching on TV. All over the world, people love football.

It's hard to believe that only 150 years ago people couldn't even agree about the rules!

And before that – there were no rules at all!

# ⚽ The World Cup

## THE FIRST WINNERS...

The first ever World Cup was held in Uruguay in 1930. Uruguay beat Argentina 4-2 in the final, which was held in the Centenario Stadium in Montevideo.

## ...AND THE MOST RECENT WINNERS

In 2002 the World Cup was played in South Korea and Japan. Brazil beat Germany 2-0 in the final. It was the seventh time they had appeared in the final, and the fifth time they had won the trophy – that's more than any other country.

## MOST GOALS IN A MATCH

Oleg Salenko of Russia scored 5 goals against Cameroon in 1994.

## THE BIGGEST CROWD FOR THE FINAL

174,000 people watched Brazil play Uruguay in the Maracana Stadium in Rio De Janeiro in 1950.

## BEST ALL-TIME WORLD CUP GOALSCORER

Gerd Muller of Germany scored 14 goals in the 1970 and 1974 competitions.

## PENALTY SHOOTOUTS

Just one final has been decided by penalties – the 1994 final between Brazil and Italy in Pasadena USA. Brazil won 3-2.

## HAT TRICKS

45 players have scored World Cup hat tricks, but only 5 players have scored two hat tricks in World Cup matches. They are: Sandor Kocsis (Hungary) in 1954, Max Morlock (France) in 1954, Just Fontaine (France) in 1958, Gerd Muller (Germany) in 1970, and Gabriel Batistuta (Argentina) in 1994 and 1998.

⬆ This is the World Cup

## International superstars

### Pele (Edson Arantes do Nascimento)

Pele played his first World Cup match when he was only 17 years old. He helped Brazil to win the World Cup three times and during his career he scored 77 goals.

# ⚽ No rules

Seven hundred years ago in England, football was a dangerous game. Hundreds of people played in the same match. They chased a ball through streets and fields. They chased it across rivers and over fences. They pushed each other too. Sometimes people were hurt, and sometimes they were killed.

➔ Football 700 years ago — a dangerous game!

The game was so dangerous that King Richard II said, 'Enough!' And football was banned.

But as the years passed, people began to play again. Football was still a dangerous game, but people loved it! And after hundreds of years, they began to think of some rules.

# ⚽ Too many rules!

At Cambridge University, 150 years ago, there were people from lots of different schools. They tried to play football together. Some players picked the ball up with their hands. Other players hacked each other's legs.

'You can't do that,' they yelled at each other. 'It's cheating!'

They all knew some rules, but they were different rules! They argued about everything. They even argued about the ball.

➔ A football team 100 years ago

'It's round,' some people said.

'No it's not. It's oval.'

At last, they all agreed. They wrote the rules down. Now people from all over Britain could play football together.

# ⚽ England and Scotland

Football in England was still a simple game. When a player got the ball, he tried to keep it. He dribbled. He ran and ran until he scored, or until someone tackled him. And the tackles were rough. Players loved to charge each other with their shoulders!

Then, in Scotland, people thought of a new way to play. They passed the ball to each other. They controlled the ball carefully. By the time someone came to tackle them, they had passed the ball to someone else! Good teams still play the same way today, although players still dribble – and some still shoulder-charge too!

# International superstars

## Diego Maradona

Maradona was one of the best players ever, but he sometimes got into trouble. He helped Argentina to win the World Cup in 1986, but in the quarter finals he used his hand to score a goal!

A women's football match in the UK

# ⚽ A game for everyone

People all over the world love playing football. They play in the deserts, in the mountains and on the beaches. Some people play in giant stadiums, and others play in the street. Some people wear expensive boots, and others play in bare feet. Old people play football, and so do little children. Two hundred and forty million men and women play in football teams all over the world.

# Did you know...

There are more than 1.5 million football teams in the world.

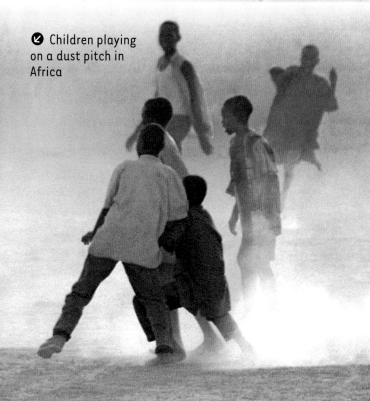

🡗 Children playing on a dust pitch in Africa

# ⚽ Football strips

Football teams wear special clothes so that they can see who is on their side when they are playing. The clothes are called strips. The goalkeeper must wear a different colour from everyone else. Here are some famous football strips.

↖ Manchester United

↗ Liverpool

↖ Celtic

↗ Inter Milan

● Juventus

● Barcelona

Fashions change in football clothes. Sometimes shorts have been long... and sometimes they have been short! Sometimes shirts have had long sleeves and collars, but now some shirts have no sleeves at all!

● Cameroon

## International superstars

### Mariel Margaret 'Mia' Hamm

Mia Hamm scored more than 100 goals for the USA, and helped them to win both the Olympic Games and World Cup during the 1990s.

# Learning to play

Whether you are the most famous footballer in the world, or a barefoot child, you still need to practise the same skills.

**can you...**

run fast with the ball at your feet?

**can you...**

control the ball instantly with your feet, your thighs, and your chest?

**can you...**

pass the ball accurately?

**can you...**

head the ball?

**can you...**

tackle safely?

**can you...**

shoot hard and straight?

Yes? Then it's time for a match.

# ⚽ Attacking...

To win a match, you must score more goals than the other team. You must attack, but defenders try to tackle you. So how can you get past them?

Here are some good ways to do it...

Pass the ball to a friend. While you race past the defender, your friend passes back to you. The defender is beaten!

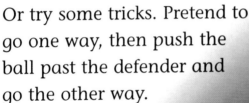

Or try some tricks. Pretend to go one way, then push the ball past the defender and go the other way.

Maybe you can even push the ball through the defender's legs!

You're past the defender, but there's still the goalkeeper to beat. Shoot hard and low, and even the best goalkeeper might not save your shot.

# ...and defending

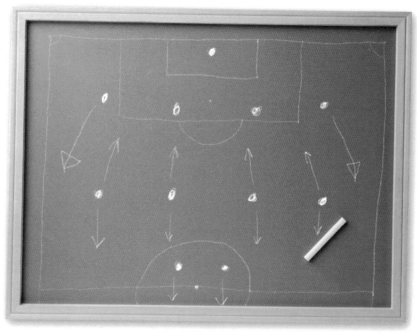

🡒 Football teams use chalkboards
to work out the best way to play

In a football team, everyone has their
own special job to do. Defenders try to
stop the other team from scoring. They
stop the other team's passes. They
tackle them, and they try not to be
fooled by the attacker's tricks!

Midfielders work hardest of all. They race back to help the defenders, and race forward to help the attackers. Behind everyone is the goalkeeper.

The goalkeeper has a lonely and difficult job. Most of the time, he stands and waits. But when an attack comes, he must be ready to leap…

or *punch...*

or **catch**…

or kick!

A goalkeeper has to be brave, too. He has to be ready to dive at the attacker's feet. Football can still be a dangerous game.

#  Foul!

The rules of football are the same for everyone, but sometimes people break the rules. Sometimes they foul!

The scores are level. An attacker races past one defender. Two more are ahead of him. He flicks the ball past them. He's beaten them. He's going to score! Then a defender stretches out his leg – and trips him! The attacker falls flat on his face, and the referee blows his whistle. '**Foul!**' he says.

He writes the defender's name in his notebook and shows him a yellow card. If the defender fouls again, he may show him a red card, and send him off the pitch. It's the referee's job to make sure the game is fair and safe.

# Dreams

In Africa, a boy is juggling a football.
He keeps it in the air with his bare feet.

In England, a boy runs on to the pitch.
He's going to play his first game for the
school team.

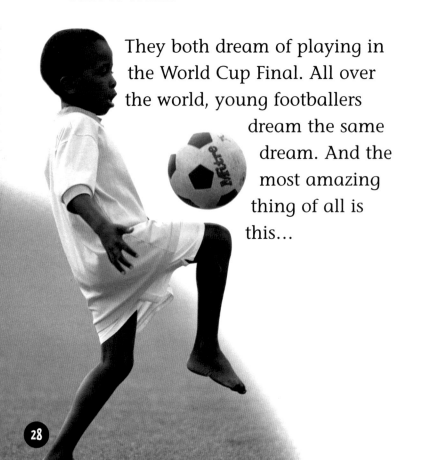

They both dream of playing in
the World Cup Final. All over
the world, young footballers
dream the same
dream. And the
most amazing
thing of all is
this...

...for some of them,
the dream will come true.

# Glossary

**attacker** Attackers try to get the ball close to the goal, and to score if they can. **24, 25**

**defender** Defenders try to stop the other team from scoring and pass the ball forward to midfielders and attackers. **4, 22, 24, 25, 27**

**dribble** When you dribble you run past other players with the ball at your feet. **14**

**foul** If you break the rules of football then you commit a foul. **26, 27**

**midfielder** A midfielder plays in the part of the pitch between attackers and defenders, and helps with both attacking and defending. **25**

**shoulder-charge** When you shoulder-charge you use your shoulder to push another player's shoulder. **14**

**stadium** A stadium is a field with rows of seats around it where football matches are played.

**6, 8, 16**

**striker** A striker is an attacking player whose special job is to score goals. **4**

**tackle** When you tackle another player you try to get the ball away from them. **14, 21**

# Reading Together

**Oxford Reds** have been written by leading children's authors who have a passion for particular non-fiction subjects. So as well as up-to-date information, fascinating facts and stunning pictures, these books provide powerful writing which draws the reader into the text.

**Oxford Reds** are written in simple language, checked by educational advisors. There is plenty of repetition of words and phrases, and all technical words are explained. They are an ideal vehicle for helping your child develop a love of reading – by building fluency, confidence and enjoyment.

You can help your child by reading the first few pages out loud, then encourage him or her to continue alone. You could share the reading by taking turns to read a page or two. Or you could read the whole book aloud, so your child knows it well before tackling it alone.

**Oxford Reds** will help your child develop a love of reading and a lasting curiosity about the world we live in.

**Sue Palmer**
*Writer and Literacy Consultant*